Cooking
TOGETHER

Real Food for the Whole Family

Cooking
TOGETHER
SARA BEGNER

SKYHORSE PUBLISHING

Skyhorse Publishing books may be purchased in bulk at special discounts for
sales promotion, corporate gifts, fund-raising, or educational purposes. Special
editions can also be created to specifications. For details, contact the Special
Sales Department, Skyhorse Publishing, 307 West 36th Street, 11th Floor, New
York, NY 10018 or info@skyhorsepublishing.com.

Skyhorse® and Skyhorse Publishing® are registered trademarks of Skyhorse
Publishing, Inc.®, a Delaware corporation.

Visit our website at www.skyhorsepublishing.com.

10 9 8 7 6 5 4 3 2 1

Library of Congress Cataloging-in-Publication Data
Begner, Sara.
Cooking together : real food for the whole family / Sara Begner.
     p. cm.
ISBN 978-1-61608-593-3 (hardcover : alk. paper)
1. Cooking. 2. Children--Nutrition. I. Title.
TX714.B3878 2012
641.5--dc23
                          2012020481]

Printed in China

TABLE OF CONTENTS

FREE YOUR MIND IN THE KITCHEN

How can I get my seven-year-old into the kitchen when *Star Wars* Legos are more tempting? What can I do when the children consistently refuse to eat anything that even resembles a vegetable, at a time when the stress around what we eat only grows? Is the only solution for some peace and quiet around the kitchen table to give in and allow dinner to consist of macaroni and hot dogs?

No, the answer is a clear no. Food is pleasure and the moment around the dinner table should be the highlight of the day, not the other way around. No new cooking skills, no magic tricks, no strange ingredients are needed. The recipe is simple:

AWAKEN THE APPETITE!
The key is to rethink the concepts. Let the children be a part of and control the process, let them in and make the kitchen the most fun room of the house. Take the roll of a mentor instead of being in charge. Give

yourself a well needed break from stressing about food and realize that sometimes a sandwich and a glass of milk can be a dinner too.

CHOOSE TOGETHER! Let the children decide what the food should taste like. Crispy is good—then we will bread the fish with seeds and nuts. Explain what food does for your body and how it works. Children are curious.

COOK TOGETHER! There is so much more to cooking than just hot pans and frying. Whipping, cracking eggs, and measuring ingredients are also a part of cooking. Let the scissors become the most important tool of the kitchen, as most things can actually be cut. Let go of control and be messy.

TASTE TOGETHER! Children's sense of taste is immature and it takes at least ten tries before a new flavor is established. Do not give up, have patience. Choose the flavor of food depending on what is familiar. Forget about fennel and saffron. Just ask if the soup should taste like licorice or saffron buns.

This is the cookbook that makes everybody long for the kitchen table!

DINNER PEACE

What should children really eat? What happens if they completely refuse vegetables? And how long will they survive eating pasta with butter?

My best advice is to relax. They do not have to eat everything; allow things to be rejected. They probably do not eat as unvaryingly as you think if you consider that the plate model can be provided during a week instead of daily. One vegetable a week is better than none at all. But most of all: Allow it to take time. Ten tries of tasting is sometimes needed for children to accept a new flavor. Hang in there, because even the most stubborn child usually tires at some point.

My next best advice for more joy around food is simple: Motivate the children and tell them what the food will do for your body. How would Zlatan have the strength to score if he only ate pasta? Make it cool to fill up on food that makes you feel good. Let the children cook with you and make decisions in the kitchen. What you make yourself always tastes the best!

'Fish

THE SAFFRON FISH ONLY SWIMS IN CALM WATERS

Never underestimate the presentation of a dish. Especially not
with a critical younger audience. Some playfulness makes a huge
difference. Fish is the best fast-food, and there are two important
rules that you should always follow: Do not cook it too long, and
use plenty of salt.

SALMON SOUP WITH SAFFRON

Servings: 4
Time: 20 minutes

2 tbsp olive oil (30 mL)
1 onion, chopped
2 cloves of garlic, chopped
1 fennel, tended, chopped
2-4 carrots, sliced
3 tbsp fish stock (45 mL)
1 can whole tomatoes (14 oz)
3 cups water (700 mL)
¾ cup white wine (200 mL)
¾ cup cream (200 mL)
1 pinch saffron (0.5 mL)
1 ½ tsp salt (4 g)
½ tsp black pepper (1 g)
17 oz. salmon filet cut into cubes (500 g)

DILL CREAM
¾ cup créme fraiche (200 mL)
½ cup dill, chopped (100 g)
1 lemon, grated zest
salt and pepper

Heat oil in a pot and fry onion, fennel, and carrot for a few minutes without bringing color to them. Add stock, tomatoes, water, wine, and cream. Let it boil for 5-7 minutes. Add saffron, salt, pepper, and salmon. Then let the soup sit for a few minutes until the salmon is done. Mix the ingredients for the dill cream and serve with the soup.

– What is for dinner?

– Fish?

– Oh no!

– Oven-baked cod

– I do not eat cod!

– What about saffron-bun fish?

– Dibs on cooking it!

With a meat thermometer, there is no doubt about it—the salmon is perfect at 125° F.

SALMON SATISFACTION

Satisfaction because you can flavor it with everything, from feta cheese to ginger. Satisfaction because it takes care of itself in the oven. Satisfaction because it turns out absolutely delicious.

Vary the taste and put in red pesto, green pesto with extra basil, tapenade feta cheese, cantadou with horseradish and grated lemon peel, brie, wrap it in bacon, or put it in barbecue spices. Do not forget to use enough salt and pepper. Put it in the oven at 350°F for 12-13 minutes and out comes the best luxury dinner.

A family that is not scared of spicy flavors can cook its salmon with chili, ginger, and lime.

SALMON WITH GINGER, CHILI, AND LIME

Servings: 6-10
Preheat oven to 350°F
Time: 10 minutes prep, 20-25 minutes cooking

25 oz. pak choi, coarsely chopped (700 g)
5 scallions, chopped
1 piece of salmon (35-53 oz./1-1 ½ kg)
3 tbsp honey (45 mL)
1 tbsp fresh ginger, grated (1 g)
1 chili without seeds, chopped
½ lime, juice
½ lime in thin slices
⅓ cup sesame seeds (50 g)

Put the pak choi and scallions in a spacious oven dish. Cut the skin from the salmon and place the fish on the greens. Sprinkle salt on the fish and greens. Mix honey, ginger, chili, and lime juice and brush it onto the fish. Put the slices of lime on the salmon and sprinkle sesame seeds on it. Bake in the middle of the oven until the thickest part of the salmon has an inner temperature of 125°F, about 20-25 minutes.

ALMOND CRUSTED POLLACK

Servings: 5
Preheat oven to 350°F
Time: 10 minutes prep, 15-20 minutes in the oven

26 oz. pollack filet (750 g)
salt and black pepper
2 cups parsley, chopped (300 g)
1 ⅓ cup almonds, chopped (200 g)
3 ½ oz. butter, room temperature (100 g)
1 lemon, grated peel and juice

9 oz. broccoli florets (250 g)
26 oz. cauliflower florets (750 g)
salt
melted butter

Place the pollack in a greased oven dish. Use plenty of salt and pepper. Mix together parsley, almonds, butter, and lemon. Spread the mixture on the fish. Bake in the middle of the oven until the thickest part of the pollack has an inner temperature of 135 °F, about 15-20 minutes.

Boil broccoli and cauliflower in salted water. Serve the greens with the pollack and melted butter.

Put the fish in the fridge in the morning so it is perfectly defrosted when it is time for dinner.

ICE-COLD FRIENDS
Sometimes a frozen package of fish is all you need to strike back against a dinner panic. Defrost, put on a crust filled with rich flavors, and enjoy.

15

MORE BREAD

Seeds, coconut, taco shells, cheese, or cornflake crumbs. Crunchy is tasty, and homemade fish sticks will surely charm the most stubborn fish opposer. How to do it? See next page!

BREADED FISH

Servings: 4
Time: 20 minutes

Bread fish with sunflower seeds, pumpkin seeds, black or white sesame seeds, coconut flakes, parmesan, oats, fresh or dried herbs, almond, melon seeds, cornflakes, and grated lemon zest.

20 oz. cod, blue grenadier, pollack, or haddock (600 g)
1-1 ½ tsp salt (3-4 g)
1 ¼ cup flour (150 g)
2 eggs, beat
about 1 ½ cup crumbs by choice

Frying
4 tbsp butter or oil (60 mL)

Cut the fish into even pieces. Salt them on all sides or mix the salt with the flour. First, turn the pieces of fish in the flour, then in the beaten eggs, and finally in the crumbs you have chosen. Fry the fish on medium heat until the breading is golden brown, about 2-3 minutes on each side. The time varies depending on how thick the fish is.

Tasty sauces to have with fried fish: tzatziki (p. 21), avocado dip (p. 36), tomato salsa (p. 41), coleslaw (p. 40), ajvar yogurt (p. 40), cucumber sauce (p. 40), Dijon sauce (p. 41), or lemon aioli (p. 99).

Tasty with the sticks: stir-fried vegetables, noodles, mashed potatoes, and yogurt sauce.

18

19

SALMON BURGER WITH TZATZIKI

Servings: 6-8 pieces
Time: 20 minutes

20 oz. skinned and boned salmon (600 g)
½ red onion, finely chopped
1 tbsp Dijon mustard (15 mL)
1 tsp salt (3 g)
½ tsp black pepper (1 g)

Frying
2 tbsp butter or olive oil (30 mL)

Quickly mix the salmon in a food processor until it is in small pieces. Mix all the ingredients and shape into six or eight burgers. Heat some butter or oil in a frying pan and fry the burgers at a medium temperature, about 3 minutes on each side.

Serve with tzatziki, hamburger rolls, salad, onion rings, and tomato.

Fast-food

Who said that burgers can only be made from meat? Mix the fish and fry until the burgers have a nice color and make the yogurt sauce. What are you waiting for? Fish is the best fast food!

TZATZIKI

½ cucumber
¾ cup neutral yogurt (200 mL)
2 garlic cloves, pressed
½ tsp salt (1 g)
black pepper
olive oil

Grate the cucumber and press as much liquid as you can from it. Mix cucumber, yogurt, garlic, salt and pepper, and stir some olive oil into the mixture.

Other dips to serve with the burger: lemon aioli (p. 99), hummus (p. 40), avocado dip (p. 36), and cucumber sauce (p. 40).

FISH PATTIES, NOODLE SALAD, AND MANGO CHUTNEY YOGURT

Servings: 4
Time: 30 minutes

20 oz. skinned and boned cod filet (or blue grenadier, haddock, or pollack) (600 g)
1 tbsp lemongrass, finely sliced (10 g)
2/3 cup scallions, finely chopped (100 g)
1 tbsp fresh ginger, grated (10 g)
1 tsp salt (3 g)
2 egg whites, beaten

Frying
3 tbsp sunflower seed oil or other neutral oil (45 mL)

NOODLE SALAD
4 ½ oz. rice noodles (125 g)
1 tbsp sunflower seed oil or other neutral oil (15 mL)
½ red chili (or color by choice), seeded, finely chopped
2 garlic cloves, finely chopped
9 oz. broccoli florets (250 g)
3 ½ oz. white cabbage, finely shredded (100 g)
1 red bell pepper, sliced
2 tbsp sweet chili sauce (30 mL)
1 lime
1 tbsp fish sauce (15 mL)
1/3 cup fresh coriander, chopped (50 g)

MANGO CHUTNEY YOGURT
½ cup neutral yogurt (10 mL)
½ cup mango chutney (100 mL)
1 lime, grated peel and juice
salt flakes

Quickly mix the cod in a food processor until it is in small pieces. Slice the lemongrass very finely; otherwise it might have a woody taste. Mix all the ingredients and shape into 8 patties. Heat the oil in a frying pan and fry the patties on medium heat, about 3 minutes on each side.

Cook the noodles according to instructions on the package. Heat the oil in a wok pan and fry chili and garlic for about a minute. Add broccoli and white cabbage, and fry on medium heat for a few minutes. Add noodles, sweet chili sauce, lime juice, fish sauce, and coriander.

Mix yogurt, chutney, and lime, adding salt to taste.

FISH PATTIES ♥ NOODLES

When children-friendly and adult treats walk hand-in-hand, it makes me extremely happy. If the children want "natural noodles" and a sample of the chutney yogurt, say okay.

23

Pizza

MEATBALL PIZZA, ANYONE?

Pizza is always a crowd pleaser. The dough is ridiculously simple to make and rises while you take care of bringing out all the flavors. The secret behind the best pizza is to keep the oven at a high temperature, while using a very hot baking sheet and allowing all to choose their favorite toppings.

PIZZA

Servings: 1 pizza
Preheat oven to 450-500° F
Time: 20 minutes prep, 30 minutes to rise,
15-20 minutes in the oven

⅓ oz. yeast (10 g)
1 cup water (250 mL)
½ tsp salt (1 g)
**4 cups flour + flour for rolling out the
    dough (480 g)**

**1 batch tomato sauce, onion sauce, or
    both (p 28-29)**
filling
aged cheese or mozzarella, grated

Dissolve the yeast in water, add the other
ingredients in, and stir into a sticky dough
by using a wooden spoon. Let it rise under
a baking cloth for 30 minutes.

Place a baking sheet in the warm oven.
Place the dough on a floured table. Roll,
pull, or part the dough until it is as thin as
you want it to be.

Place the dough on parchment baking
paper. Spread tomato or onion sauce over
it, or vary with both. Place the filling on
the pizza and sprinkle with cheese (unless
you already used it as filling).

Take out the hot baking sheet and pull
the pizza onto it by using the parchment
baking paper. Bake in the middle of the
oven until the cheese melts and has a nice
color, about 15-20 minutes.

The right dough

Whatever topping you choose for your pizza, it all starts with the dough.

CHEWY DOUGH = SKIMP ON THE FLOUR and be more generous when it is time to roll out the dough.

To spin the pizza on your finger is for a more advanced cook. Take a shortcut and spin it with your hands instead. Round, square, or completely irregular, the taste is all that counts.

Mix a quick adult sauce completely without tomatoes. Just use garlic, wine, oregano, and olive oil—yummy.

feta cheese
olives

salami
hot peppers

sardines, onion,
cherry tomatoes

minced meat
pineapple

TOMATO SAUCE

Time: 20 minutes

2 tbsp olive oil (30 mL)
½ yellow onion, finely chopped
2 garlic cloves, finely chopped
1 can (14 oz.) crushed tomatoes (400 g)
1 tsp salt (3 g)
½ tsp black pepper (1 g)
2 tbsp chili sauce (30 mL)
2 tsp dried thyme or oregano (6 g)

Heat the oil in a pan and fry the onion
for a minute without bringing color to it.
Add the rest of the ingredients and
let the sauce simmer until it thickens,
about 10-15 minutes.

goat cheese
walnuts

shrimp
clams

bananas
peanuts

ONION SAUCE

Time: 10 minutes

½ cup olive oil (100 mL)
1 yellow onion, coarsely chopped
2-3 garlic cloves, coarsely chopped
½ cup white wine
1 tsp salt (3 g)
½ tsp black pepper (1 g)
2 tsp dried oregano (6 g)

Heat the oil in a pan and fry the onion
for a minute without bringing color to
it. Add the rest of the ingredients and
simmer until the onion is soft, about
5 minutes. Mix with a hand blender until
smooth.

Minced Meat

SPEED UP THE MINCE

The Spaniards add finely chopped spicy sausages in theirs. The Italians fill theirs up with parmesan and lemon. The Greeks use oregano and mint, while the Chinese prefer to eat it with sweet-and-sour sauce. Meatballs are made all over the world and the possibilities with minced meat are endless. Here are the best dinners for the week.

MINCE SKEWERS WITH RED CABBAGE AND PINE NUTS

Servings: 10-12 skewers
Time: 30 minutes

10-12 soaked wooden skewers, 10 inches long
17 ½ oz. beef, minced (500 g)
3 garlic cloves, pressed
1 tsp ground cinnamon (3 g)
1 tsp ground cumin (3 g)
1 tsp cayenne pepper (3 g)
2 tsp paprika powder (6 g)
1 ½ tsp salt (4 g)
½ cup Turkish and Greek yogurt (100 mL)

For frying
2 tbsp butter or olive oil (30 mL)

RED CABBAGE SALAD
¼ red cabbage head
2 tbsp red wine vinegar (30 mL)
1 tbsp sugar (10 g)
1 tbsp salt flakes (10 g)

1 ¾ oz. pine nuts, roasted (50 g)
Turkish and Greek yogurt or hummus
10-12 pieces of pita bread

Mix minced beef, garlic, spices, and yogurt into an even batter. Squeeze minced beef so it sticks to the skewers. Heat butter or oil in a large frying pan and fry the minced skewers until they have a nice color, a few minutes altogether.

Shred the red cabbage finely by using a cheese slicer or a food processor. Mix vinegar, sugar, and salt and mix with the minced meat.

Serve the skewers and salad in pita bread with pine nuts and yogurt or hummus (p. 40).

FLAVOR FRIENDS FOR THE MINCE

No matter what shape you plan for the minced meat, it needs flavor friends. Mix it with grated lemon zest, green pepper, sun-dried tomatoes, spicy sausage, fresh herbs of choice, feta cheese, olives, capers, pesto, parmesan, and ajvar relish. Create your own favorites and remember to use all the yummy sides.

MOM'S MEATLOAF WITH ONION SOUP AND BACON

Servings: 8
Preheat oven to 400° F
Time: 15 minutes prep, 40 minutes in the oven

⅔ cup oats, bread crumbs (optional) (100 g)
2 eggs
1 ¼ cup sour cream (300 mL)
2 ½ pounds minced beef (1 kg)
1 package powdered onion soup (1.4 oz./40 g)
½ tsp black pepper (1 g)
olive oil
5 oz. bacon slices (140 g)

28 oz. potatoes, halved (800 g)
salt flakes
black pepper
rosemary twigs
olive oil

Mix oats, eggs, sour cream, minced beef, onion powder, and black pepper. Grease a spacious baking pan with olive oil, and place the minced beef in and shape into a loaf.

Place potatoes around the loaf, add salt, pepper, and rosemary twigs, and drizzle with olive oil. Bake in the middle of the oven for about 40 minutes.

Serve with a cold sauce (Dijon sauce, for example: p. 41).

ENHANCE THE LOAF
Meatloaf wakes up childhood memories, but now it is time for version 2.0. Season with anything you like and cook it the night before to prepare for dinner the next day.

Make a large batch and the loaf will make two dinners.
Day 1: Warm with potatoes,
Day 2: Cold on a sandwich or in the lunch box. This dish is my mother's trick, and evokes nostalgia from the '80s.

AJVAR BURGERS

Servings: 6 pieces
Time: 20 minutes

17 ½ oz. minced beef (500 g)
½ cup ajvar relish, mild or spicy
(100 mL)
½-1 tsp salt (1-3 g)
6-12 slices of bread

For frying
2 tbsp butter + some for the bread
   slices (30 g)

Mix minced beef, ajvar, salt, and pep-per. Shape into 6 patties. Heat up some butter in a frying pan and fry the burger on medium heat, about 3-4 minutes on each side. If needed, heat up some more butter and fry the bread slices. You can also grill the bread in a pan or toaster. Compose your own burger with the toppings you like—for instance, lettuce, tomato, cheese, bacon, avocado, pep-peroni, and root vegetable chips.

Mix ajvar relish in the minced beef for a burger with sting.

THE HEIGHT OF HAPPINESS
Flatten the minced beef and fry or grill. Be gen-erous with sides and let everyone create their own burgers. Burgers are self-service at its best.

AVOCADO DIP

Time: 5 minutes

2 avocados, pitted
½ lemon, grated zest and juice
½ cup neutral yogurt (100 mL)
2 garlic cloves, pressed
salt
pepper

Place the avocado pulp in a bowl together with lemon, yogurt, and garlic. Mix with a hand blender or fork. Add salt and pepper to taste.

Pippi with a twist!

Fast, homemade, and tasty: Mayonnaise, yogurt, and cucumber relish.

CHICKEN BURGERS

Servings: 4-5 pieces
Time: 15 minutes

14 oz. minced chicken (400 g)
⅔ cup scallions, chopped (100 g)
1 tbsp fresh salvia, chopped or 1 tsp dried (10/3 g)
1 tbsp squeezed lemon (15 mL)
½ lemon, zest
1 tsp salt (3 g)
black pepper

For frying
2 tbsp butter (30 g)

Mix all the ingredients and shape the batter into 4 or 5 burgers. Heat butter in a frying pan and fry the burgers on medium to low heat, about 4-5 minutes on each side. Serve with a dip; see p. 40-41, and your favorite toppings.

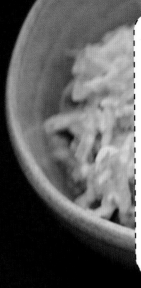

COLESLAW

Time: 10 minutes

10 ½ oz. white cabbage (300 g)
7 oz. carrot, grated (200 g)
2 tart apples, cored and grated
¾ cup yogurt (200 mL)
salt
pepper

Grate the white cabbage with a grater, shave it with a cheese slicer, or shred it in a food processor. Mix all the ingredients and add salt and pepper to taste.

AJVAR YOGURT

Time: 1 minute

¾ cup ajvar relish, mild or spicy (200 mL)
⅔ cup yogurt (150 mL)

Mix the ingredients.

CUCUMBER SAUCE

Time: 2 minutes

¾ Turkish or Greek yogurt (200 mL)
1 cup cucumber relish (150 mL)
¼ cup mayonnaise (50 mL)

Mix the ingredients.

...TY DIPS

...day luxury with many extra dips and ...s. Voilà, a new world has landed on your

HUMMUS

Time: 5 minutes

28 oz. (2 cans) cooked chickpeas (800 g)
2 garlic cloves
1 ½ tbsp tahini with salt (22.5 mL)
4 tbsp lemon juice (60 mL)
½ tsp salt (1 g)
½ cup olive oil (100 mL)

Rinse the chickpeas with cold water in a colander and drain. Mix chickpeas, garlic, tahini, lemon juice, and salt in a food processor. Pour the oil in while the food processor is mixing.

If using tahini without salt, add 1-1 ½ tsp salt.

TOMATO SALSA

Time: 5 minutes

2 tomatoes, finely chopped
½ red onion, finely chopped
⅔ cup crushed tomatoes from a can
 (100 g)
⅓ cup fresh basil, shredded in strips
 (50 g)
1 tsp sugar (3 g)
1 tsp salt (3 g)
black pepper
optional: chili, seeded, finely chopped

Mix all the ingredients. Add red chili
if you want to add some sting to the
salsa, green chili if you really want
some sting.

DIJON SAUCE

Time: 2 minutes

¾ cup crème fraiche (200 mL)
1 ½ tsp Dijon mustard (7.5 mL)
grated lemon zest
1 tsp olive oil (5 mL)
salt and pepper

Mix crème fraiche, mustard, lemon
zest, and oil. Add salt and pepper to
taste.

Good music is a must. It adds a better swing to the rolling.

START A MEATBALL FACTORY
Few things give you the same shivers of pleasure as opening the freezer and finding your own homemade meatballs. Roll, fry, and freeze is my motto.

If you get tired of anything that is even close to frying, you can freeze the meatballs raw in portion packages and fry them when it's time for dinner.

Mix the sauce before you add the meatballs, but do it in a sauce pan with high sides —otherwise it will splash everywhere.

LAMB MEATBALLS IN AUBERGINE AND TOMATO SAUCE

Servings: 4
Time: 30 minutes

14 oz. minced lamb (400 g)
3 ½ oz. feta cheese, crumbled (100 g)
⅔ cup pitted, chopped black olives (100 g)
½ red onion, chopped
½ cup neutral yogurt (100 mL)
pepper

For frying
2 tbsp butter (30 g)

AUBERGINE AND TOMATO SAUCE
2 tbsp olive oil (45 mL)
14 oz. aubergine, chopped (400 g)
1 red onion, chopped
2 garlic cloves, chopped
1 ⅔ cup water (400 mL)
1 can crushed tomatoes (14 oz./400 g)
½ tbsp honey (7.5 mL)
salt and black pepper

Start with the sauce: Heat the oil and fry the aubergine and onion on high heat for about 10 minutes. Add water, tomatoes, honey, salt, and pepper. Let simmer.

   Mix the minced lamb with the rest of the ingredients and roll into meatballs. Heat some butter in a frying pan and fry the meatballs all around. Then place them in the sauce and let them finish cooking. Serve with pasta.

SPAGHETTI AND BOLOGNESE

Servings: 4
Time: 20-30 minutes

½ batch onion mixture
17 ½ oz. beef or mixed minced meat (500 g)
1 can (14 oz.) crushed tomatoes (400 g)
1 tbsp meat stock (15 mL)
¼ cup cream (50 mL)
1 tsp dried oregano (3 g)
salt
pepper

10 ½ oz. spaghetti (300 g)
1 tbsp olive oil (15 mL)
shaved parmesan
fresh basil
black pepper

Fry the onion mix and minced meat in a hot frying pan while stirring. Add tomatoes, stock, cream, and oregano, adding salt and pepper to taste. Let simmer for 10-20 minutes. Boil spaghetti according to the instructions on the package and mix oil with the cooked, drained spaghetti. Garnish with parmesan, basil, and black pepper if you want to.

Topping makes a difference: Lavish with fresh parmesan and basil

ONION MIXTURE

Serving: Enough for 2 ½ pounds of minced meat (1 kg)
Time: 5 minutes

2 yellow onions in pieces
3 garlic cloves
²/₃ cup olive oil (150 mL)

Place the ingredients in a container with high sides. Mix with a hand blender until onion and oil turn into a smooth paste.

Free from onion pieces
It is often the pieces, not the flavor in itself, that cause a problem when using onion in your food. Mix garlic and onion very finely and the problem is quickly solved.

44

SALISBURY STEAK WITH ONION AND MASHED POTATOES

Servings: 4
Times: 30 minutes

½ cup water (100 mL)
⅔ cup oats (100 g)
17 ½ oz. minced beef (500 g)
1 egg
1 tsp salt (3 g)
½ tsp black pepper (1 g)
2 sliced onions, yellow or red or both

3-4 tbsp butter for frying (45-60 g)

MASHED POTATOES
2 ⅓ pounds floury potatoes, cut into pieces (1 kg)
1 ¼ cup milk (250-300 mL)
1-2 tbsp butter (15-30 g)
salt
pepper

Mix water and oats and let swell for a few minutes. Add minced beef, egg, salt, and pepper. Work the ingredients together and form about 10 patties. Heat some butter in a frying pan. Fry the patties on medium heat and then finish by frying on low heat for about 4 minutes on each side. Then fry the onion in some butter until soft. Another option is to add 1/4 cup water and let simmer.

MASHED POTATOES
Boil the potatoes in lightly salted water. Heat the milk in a different sauce pan. Pour off the water from the potatoes and mash with an electric mixer. Add milk and whip until it reaches the desired texture. Whip butter into the mashed potatoes and add salt and pepper to taste.

Serve fried, sliced onion with the Salisbury steak and the whole family will be happy.

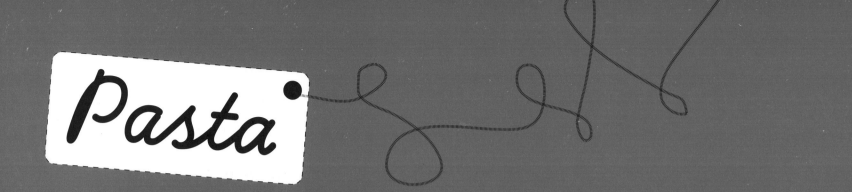

I LOVE PASTA

Pasta is just like a stew: Throw in whatever you have at home and in a few minutes you have created a new favorite dish. Do not throw away leftover pasta. Instead, mix it with boiled broccoli and make a pasta gratin. Dinner for the next day is already done.

PASTA AND BROCCOLI GRATIN

Servings: 4
Preheat oven to: 400° F
Time: 15 minutes prep, 25 minutes in the oven

9 oz. pasta (250 g)
1 tbsp butter (15 g)
10 ½ oz. fresh or frozen broccoli florets (300 g)
1 ²/₃ cup milk (400 mL)
6 eggs
3 ½ oz. parmesan (100 g)
1 tsp salt (3 g)
black pepper

Boil the pasta according to instructions on the package. Grease a baking pan with butter and place the pasta and broccoli in it. Whip milk, eggs, half of the cheese, salt, and pepper together. Pour the egg mixture over the pasta and broccoli, while sprinkling with the rest of the cheese. Bake in the middle of the oven for about 25 minutes until the eggs are firm and the gratin has a nice color.

Serve with fried sausage, perhaps breakfast sausage for the children and chorizo for the adults.

SUPER BOX
Eat more broccoli, as a more nutritious vegetable can hardly be found anywhere. Briefly boil and serve with butter or add to a yummy gratin.

COOL CARBONARA

Servings: 4
Time: 20 minutes

10 ½ oz. spaghetti (300 g)
10 oz. bacon in pieces (280 g)
2 garlic cloves, pressed
4 egg yolks
½ cup cream (100 mL)
3 ½ oz. parmesan, grated (100 g)
black pepper
salt (optionally)
leafy parsley, chopped (optional)

Boil the spaghetti according to the instructions on
the package. Fry the pieces of bacon until crispy.
Stir garlic, egg yolk, cream, parmesan, and black
pepper together. Mix spaghetti, bacon, and cheese
mixture together. Add some salt and chopped
parsley if you want.

NUMBER ONE ON THE PASTA CHART
Lean back on the couch and let the children take over in the kitchen. Cool carbonara is your ace in the hole.

Save dishes and mix eggs, cream, parmesan, and garlic in the same bowl.

Safe pieces: Cut bacon with scissors instead of a knife.

49

Pillow pasta

Tortellini is fine to eat with just butter and coarsely grated parmesan. If you want to challenge your cooking skills, you can make a creamy cheese sauce and garnish it with crispy sugar snaps.

TORTELLINI WITH CHEESE SAUCE

Servings: 4
Time: 15 minutes

17 ½ oz fresh tortellini (500 g)

CHEESE SAUCE
1 tbsp butter (15 g)
½ leek, thinly sliced
1 cup milk (250 mL)
1 tbsp corn starch + 1 tbsp water (7.5 g+15 mL)
2 tbsp crème fraiche (30 mL)
½ tsp salt (1 g)
½ tsp black pepper (1 g)
2 cups aged cheese, grated (300 g)
5 ⅓ oz sugar snaps (150 g)
parsley, chopped (optionally)

Boil the tortellini according to the instructions on the package.

Warm the butter in a sauce pan and fry the leeks for a few minutes. Add the milk and bring to a boil. Add corn starch and water and stir milk and leeks into the pan. Add crème fraiche, salt and pepper, and let boil for about a minute. Remove the pan from the heat and stir cheese, sugar snaps, and parsley (optional) into the pan. Add the boiled tortellini and serve immediately.

MEATBALL SOUP (MINESTRONE WITH MEATBALLS)

Servings: 5
Time: 20 minutes (if you have premade meatballs)

2 tbsp olive oil (30 mL)
½ leek, finely sliced
2 garlic cloves, chopped
2 tbsp tomato purée (30 g)
10 ½ oz. carrots, chopped (300 g)
1 ¾ oz. celeriac, chopped (50 g)
7 oz. white cabbage, sliced (200 g)
1 ½ quart water (1 ½ liter)
2 vegetable stock cubes
1 ½ cup pasta, for example
  miniature shells (200 g)
about 20 fried meatballs
salt
black pepper

Heat oil in a big sauce pan or pot. Fry leeks and garlic for about a minute, then add tomato purée and fry for another minute. Add vegetables, water, and stock cubes. Bring to a boil and then add the pasta. Boil until the pasta is done, about 10 minutes. Add the meatballs and bring to a boil again. Add salt and pepper to taste.

Meatball soup
Meatballs that are leftovers from yesterday's dinner can actually swim. They are very exciting friends to the vegetables and pasta and fantasy is an asset in the kitchen as well.

51

SHORTCUT TO LASAGNA
Mix grated cheese, crème fraiche, milk, and organic tomatoes from a can and you have "béchamel the easy way." Fresh lasagna sheets and filling by choice. Tasty dinner!

Become the chef of the year in your kitchen and season the minced meat or chicken with taco spices.

LASAGNA WITH TACO CHICKEN

Servings: 4
Preheat oven to: 400 °F
Time: 15 minutes prep, 20-35 minutes in the oven

2 tbsp butter (30 g)
17 ½ oz. chicken breast filets, strips (500 g)
1 bag taco spice mix or your own taco spice
¼ cup water (100 mL)
1 can crushed tomatoes (14 oz./400 g)
¾ cup milk (200 mL)
¾ cup crème fraiche (200 mL)
salt and pepper
1 tbsp butter
5 ⅓ oz. fresh or dried lasagna sheets (150 g)
2 cups aged cheese, grated (300 g)

TACO SPICE
1 tbsp ground cumin (10 g)
1 tsp ground coriander (3 g)
1 tsp paprika powder (3 g)
1 tsp cayenne pepper (3 g)
2 tsp salt (6 g)
2 vegetable stock cubes
optionally 1 tsp sugar (6 g)

Heat butter in a frying pan and fry the chicken strips. Add the spice mix and water, then stir and let it simmer for a few minutes. Place tomatoes, milk, and crème fraiche in a container and mix it with a hand blender. Add salt and pepper.

Grease a baking pan. Make layers of tomato, milk, chicken, and lasagna sheets. Sprinkle with cheese and bake until the lasagna has a nice color: 20-25 minutes for fresh pasta and 30-35 minutes for dried pasta.

TACO SPICE
Grind all the ingredients in a mortar or mix them.

Chicken, minced beef, ham, or sausage—in the end, it will all taste like lasagna.

53

Food for Your Bones

HI GRANDMA, WANT TO
HAVE A CHEWING COMPETITION?

To chew is tasty, to eat with your fingers makes it even tastier. If you
also call it food for your bones, the happiness is complete. Meat with bones has
more flavor. All-in-one dishes are great in the middle of everyday stress,
but they are also the best Sunday dinners.
Because who says no to a moment of relaxation before dinnertime?

RISK-FREE GRILL
To burn pork ribs is almost impossible when they are just being heated up on the grill. Cook the bones with a little vinegar and top with a yummy, sweet glaze.

CHUTNEY-GLAZED PORK RIBS

Servings: 4
Time: 15 minutes prep, 1 hour cooking time

2 ¼ pounds thin pork ribs (1 kg)
2 quarts of water (2 liters)
2 tbsp vinegar (30 mL)
3 meat stock cubes
½ tbsp salt (1 g)
1 tsp whole black pepper (3 g)
2 yellow onions, split
⅔ cup mango chutney (150 mL)

RHUBARB CHUTNEY
3 ⅓ cups rhubarb, sliced (500 g)
¼ cup balsamic vinegar (50 mL)
1 garlic clove, chopped
½ red chili, seeded and chopped
1 cup sugar (200 g)

Split the pork ribs in two or three pieces. Bring water, vinegar, stock cubes, salt, black pepper, and onion to a boil. Add the ribs and boil for 1 hour. Pour out the water. Cut the ribs and brush them with mango chutney. Grill outside on a barbecue grill or in a grill pan without fat until the pork has a nice color.

Mix all the ingredients for the chutney in a pan and bring to a boil, about 5 minutes.

Mango chutney serves perfectly as a glaze. Season it with pressed garlic, chopped herbs, soy, oyster sauce, or chipotle pasta.

BONES THE EXPRESS WAY

Fry lamb chops with rosemary and garlic. Slice the potatoes instead of making wedges. Make a tomato salsa with avocado instead of sauce. Done!

LAMB CHOPS WITH OVEN-BAKED POTATOES AND TOMATO AND AVOCADO SALSA

Servings: 4
Preheat oven to: 450° F
Time: 20 minutes prep, 30-40 minutes in the oven

2 ½ pounds potatoes, preferably with peel (1 kg)
¼ cup olive oil (50 mL)
1- 1 ½ tbsp salt flakes (10-15 g)
1 lemon, in thick slices
2 tbsp butter (30 g)
1 tbsp olive oil (15 mL)
8 lamb chops
salt
pepper
rosemary twigs
1 garlic bulb

TOMATO AND AVOCADO SALSA
3 tomatoes, seeded and chopped
2 avocados, pitted and chopped
½ red onion, finely chopped
chopped basil leaves
1 tbsp honey (15 mL)
1 tsp squeezed lemon
salt and black pepper

Slice the potatoes in ½ inch thick slices. Place the slices in a baking pan together with oil, salt, lemon, and rosemary, making sure to stir. Leave in the oven until the potatoes have a nice color and are soft, about 30-40 minutes.

Heat some butter and oil in a frying pan. Allow the pan to become very hot. Fry the lamb chops in two turns, salt and pepper on both sides, about 2-4 minutes on each side. Add rosemary twigs and whole garlic cloves in the frying pan.

Mix the ingredients for the tomato and avocado salsa and add salt and pepper to taste.

Feta cheese + crème fraiche + chili = tasty dip

Broccoli is simple to cook but needs butter and salt to become interesting.

PORK CHOPS WITH BROCCOLI AND FETA CHEESE DIP

Servings: 2
Time: 15 minutes prep

2 tbsp oil (30 mL)
1 tbsp butter (15 g)
4 pork chops
17 ½ oz. broccoli florets (500 g)
salt
pepper

FETA CHEESE DIP
7 oz feta cheese (200 g)
¾ cup crème fraiche
½ red chili, seeded, finely chopped

Heat oil and butter in a large frying pan (or fry in two rounds in a smaller pan). Allow the pan to become very hot. Add pork chops and broccoli. Fry the pork chops for 2-4 minutes on each side, adding salt and pepper on both sides and on the broccoli. Let the broccoli fry, turning occasionally.

Mix feta cheese, crème fraiche, and chili.

FIRST TIP FOR SUCCESS
Allow the frying pan to become very hot before you add the pork chops, otherwise they will be cooked instead of fried. Pull the pan aside and let the meat rest after heating. Second tip for success: Serve with a forest of green trees.

Mashed potatoes, butter gravy, broccoli, and juicy pork chops. Yummy.

59

OSSO BUCO

Stew is not a quick dish, but requires more time. It is the bone marrow that provides the magical stew flavor. Adults can spice up the plate with a dangerously tasty gremolata.

OSSO BUCO

Servings: 4
Time: 20 minutes of prep, 1-2 hours cooking

¼ cup olive oil (50 mL)
3 garlic cloves, chopped
1 yellow onion, chopped
3 carrots, chopped (72 g)
5 ⅓ oz. celeriac, chopped (150 g)
1 can whole tomatoes (14 oz./400 g)
¾ cup white wine (200 mL)
½ cup water (100 mL)
3 tbsp veal stock (45 mL)
black pepper
2 bay laurel leaves
2 tsp dried thyme (6 g)
1 ⅓ cup flour (150 g)
1 tsp salt (3 g)
½ tsp black pepper (1 g)
2 ¼ pounds cross-cut veal shanks, sliced (1 kg)
2 tbsp butter (30 g)

GREMOLATA
1 ⅓ cup parsley, chopped (200 g)
2 garlic cloves, chopped
1 tbsp lemon zest, grated (10 g)

Heat oil in a pot. Fry onion and root vegetables for a few minutes without bringing color to it. Add tomatoes, wine, water, stock, pepper, laurel leaves, and thyme. Bring to a boil.

Mix flour, salt, and pepper on a plate, and place the veal in the mixture. Heat butter in a frying pan and brown the veal. Then place it in the tomato sauce. Place the lid on the pot and let it simmer for at least one hour, preferably one and a half to two. The meat should be tender and almost fall apart when it is done. Another option is to remove the lid and increase the heat for the last 20 minutes, which will make the sauce thicker. Add salt and pepper to taste.

Mix the ingredients for the gremolata and serve with the stew.

CHICKEN STEW

Servings: 4
Time: 20 minutes prep, 35-45 minutes of cooking

1 chicken (2 ½-3 pounds/1-1.3 kg)
2 tbsp olive oil (30 mL)
1 tbsp butter (15 g)
1 tsp salt (3 g)
black pepper
1 yellow onion, chopped
3 garlic cloves, chopped
5 oz bacon, finely sliced (140 g)
¼ cup tomato purée (50 g)
1 can crushed tomatoes (14 oz./400 g)
1 ¼ cup white wine (300 mL)
½ cup water (100 mL)
1 ½ chicken stock cubes
7 oz. pearl onion, preferably red (200 g)
2 carrots, sliced

Split the chicken into 8 pieces. Heat some oil and butter in a wok pan. Brown the chicken pieces in two rounds, adding salt and pepper. Set the pieces aside.

Fry the onion and bacon for a few minutes. Add the purée and fry for another minute. Add tomatoes, wine, water, and stock cubes. Bring to a boil and add the chicken pieces. Let simmer for 15 minutes without a lid, and then add pearl onion and carrots, and let it simmer for another 20-30 minutes. Serve with rice, potatoes, or pasta.

If you want to, save some bacon when it is fried, and sprinkle it over the finished stew.

CLEAN OUT THE VEGETABLE BOX

Fill a large baking pan with a heavenly mix of chicken drumsticks and whatever happens to be found in the refrigerator. Forgotten root vegetables, potatoes, and fresh herbs. Do not throw away anything.

CHICKEN DRUMSTICKS ● AND VEGETABLES IN THE OVEN

Servings: 4
Preheat oven to: 400° F
Time: 15 minutes prep, about 40 minutes in the oven

28 ½ oz. vegetables and root vegetables, for example: fennel, carrot, red onion, parsnip (800 g)
31 ¾ oz. chicken drumsticks (900 g)
3 tbsp mango chutney (45 mL)
3 tbsp olive oil (45 mL)
2 tbsp Kikkoman soy or other light soy (30 mL)
1 tbsp balsamic vinegar (15 mL)
1 tbsp salt flakes (10 g)
1 tsp black pepper (3 g)

GINGER YOGURT
¾ cup neutral yogurt (200 mL)
½ tbsp grated fresh ginger or ½ tsp dried (5 g/1 g)
grated lemon zest
salt and black pepper

Peel root vegetables and vegetables, cutting into pieces or strips. Place vegetables, root vegetables, and chicken in a baking pan. Mix chutney, oil, soy, and balsamic vinegar, pouring it over the pan. Add salt and pepper. Mix everything with your hands and leave in the oven until the chicken is done, about 35-40 minutes. Stir once or twice.

Mix yogurt, ginger, and lemon zest. Add salt and pepper to taste.

Entirely boneless, this roast beef still has lots of flavor. This recipe makes enough for several dinners and tastes as great as a fine steak..

Leftovers deluxe
Boil the potatoes in advance and the dinner is done in 10 minutes.

The roast beef should be room temperature before you brown it. Use a meat thermometer and let the wonderful beef sit a while before serving it = an awesome roast beef.

WHOLE ROAST BEEF WITH FETA VEGETABLES

Servings: 8
Preheat oven to: 275° F and 400° F
Time: 20 minutes prep, 2 hours in the oven

2-3 tbsp salt flakes (20-30 g)
1 ½ tbsp paprika powder (15 g)
2 tbsp rosé pepper, ground (20 g)
4 garlic cloves, pressed
4 pounds roast beef (1.8 kg)
2 tbsp butter (30 g)
1 tbsp olive oil (15 mL)
unpeeled garlic cloves
rosemary twigs

FETA VEGETABLES
1 squash, slices
3 tomatoes, pieces
2 red onions, wedges
2 red bell peppers, pieces
3 tbsp olive oil (45 mL)
salt flakes and pepper
10 ½ oz. feta cheese, crumbled (300 g)
fresh thyme, rosemary, or oregano
black olives

Mix salt, paprika powder, pepper, rosemary, and garlic. Cover the entire piece of meat with the spice mixture. Heat a frying pan until very hot. Place butter and oil in the pan and brown the roast beef. Place the roast beef in a baking pan. Place unpeeled garlic cloves and rosemary around the beef. Bake the beef in the lower part of the oven until its inner temperature is 140° F, which should take about 2 hours.

When about 30 minutes is left, place the vegetables on a baking sheet with parchment baking paper, sprinkling with oil, salt, and pepper. Place the baking sheet high up in the oven and raise the temperature to 400° F. You can also place vegetables and cheese around the beef and increase the heat.

Mix olives with the vegetables. Another option is to press the garlic out of its peel and mix it with the vegetables.

POTATO SALAD WITH COLD-CUT ROAST BEEF

Servings: 4
Time: 10 minutes prep, 30 minutes for cooking potatoes and cooling them off

VINAIGRETTE
3 tbsp olive oil (45 mL)
2 tbsp white balsamic vinegar (30 mL)
1 tsp sweet mustard (5 mL)
1 ½ tsp salt (4 g)
½ tsp black pepper (1 g)

2 ½ pounds cooked, cold potatoes, peeled (optional), in pieces (1 kg)
½ red onion, sliced
1 red bell pepper, in pieces
5 ⅓ oz. gherkins (150 g)
½ cup broth from the gherkins (100 mL)
fresh herbs, for instance parsley, thyme, oregano, or chervel

21 oz cold roast beef, sliced (600 g)

Stir the vinaigrette together and mix with potatoes, bell pepper, gherkins, and herbs. Serve with the roast beef.

Other things to season the potato salad with: sun dried tomatoes, pesto, olives, feta cheese, parmesan, arugula, baby spinach, cherry tomatoes, fresh or dried herbs, capers, scallions, leek, yellow onion, horseradish.

Picnic

OUTDOOR FOOD IS TOTALLY IN

Even if there is wind in your hair and the sun is nowhere to be seen, it is always peak season to eat outside. Food always tastes best out in the fresh air, especially when you're free to get messy. Eat outside often.

PUFF PASTRY PIEROGIES

Servings: 12 pieces
Preheat oven to: 400°F

15 oz. (1 package) puff pastry, defrosted (425 g)
5 ⅓ oz. feta cheese (150 g)
½ cup tapenade (100 g)
1 egg, beaten
sesame seeds

Roll out the puff pastry with a little flour. Cut out circles of about 4 inches in diameter. Slice or crumble feta cheese on top with a spoon of tapenade on one side of the circle. Cover with the other side and carefully press the pierogie together.

Place the pierogies on a baking sheet with parchment baking paper, brush with egg, and sprinkle with sesame seeds. Bake in the oven until they have a nice color, about 15-20 minutes.

Serve with a salad.

Fill with minced beef and make pierogies
the newest addition to your picnic basket.

Forget about the store-bought
pierogies
Ready-made puff pastry lets you skip to
the essential part of making pierogies:
the filling!

PORK PANCAKES WITH BERRIES AND APPLES

Servings: 4-6
Preheat oven to: 450° F
Time: 10 minutes prep, 35 minutes in the oven

10 ½ oz. salted pork or bacon, in pieces (300 g)
2 ⅓ cup flour (300 g)
½ tsp salt (1 g)
2 ½ cup milk (600 mL)
4 eggs

BERRIES AND APPLES
4 tart apples, peeled, cored, in pieces (500 g)
½ cup sugar (100 g)
2 tbsp lemon juice (30 mL)
4 ½ oz. frozen berries (125 g)

Place the pork or bacon pieces in a baking pan. Bake in the oven for 10-15 minutes until the pork has a nice color, stirring occasionally. Whip flour, salt, and milk into a smooth batter. Add the eggs and whip into a smooth batter again. Pour the batter over the pork and bake in the middle of the oven until the pancake is formed and has a nice color, about 25 minutes.

Bring apples, sugar, and lemon juice to a boil. Let it simmer until almost all fluid has evaporated and the apples are soft. Remove from the stove and add the berries.

Extra large pancake
Are you tired of frying pancakes?
Do what I do and pour the batter into a baking pan.

71

WRAPS WITH CHICKEN AND WHITE CABBAGE SALAD

Servings: 12 pieces
Preheat oven to: 400° F
Time: 10 minutes prep, optionally 30 minutes of steeping, 30 minutes in the oven

**1 bag tandoori spice mix or 1 batch
 homemade taco spice (p. 53)**
¾ cup neutral yogurt
31 ¾ oz. chicken breast filet (900 g)

WHITE CABBAGE SALAD
3 tbsp balsamic vinegar (45 mL)
3 tbsp olive oil (45 mL)
1 tbsp honey (15 mL)
1 tbsp squeezed lemon (15 mL)
salt and pepper
½ white cabbage head
⅔-1 ⅓ cup yellow raisins (100-200 g)
1 ⅓ cup walnuts, chopped (200 g)

12 soft wraps
**about 12 lettuce leaves, for example
romaine lettuce**

Mix the spice mix with the yogurt in a baking pan and add the chicken filets. Turn them until they are covered in spice yogurt. If you can, let the chicken sit in the refrigerator for 30 minutes. Bake the chicken in the oven until done, about 30 minutes. Let it cool and then cut the filets into thin slices.

 Mix vinegar, oil, honey, pressed garlic, lemon, salt, and pepper in a bowl that fits the white cabbage. Remove the stem of the cabbage and slice with a cheese slicer, in a food processor, or by hand. Mix vinaigrette, raisins, and walnuts.

 The salad should stay fresh for several days in the refrigerator. Add the nuts right before serving, otherwise they will turn soft.

WRAP A WRAP
Ham, chicken, ketchup, meatballs, and breaded fish. Anything can be wrapped. If you want, you can equip your wrap with extra carrots, salad, or coleslaw.

Carrot sticks and bell pepper wedges come along on the picnic.

EGG SANDWICHES ●

Servings: 4
Time: 10 minutes prep

2 tbsp butter (30 g)
4 eggs
salt and black pepper
mayonnaise for the bread
8 slices bread
2 tomatoes, sliced
4-8 lettuce leaves

Melt the butter in a frying pan and fry
the eggs. Add salt and pepper. Spread
the mayonnaise on the bread slices;
add an egg, tomato slices, and lettuce
leaves. Finish with another slice of
bread and package the sandwich in a
napkin or greaseproof paper.

FRUIT SKEWERS

wooden skewers
different fruit, for example pineapple, peaches, lemon,
strawberries

Peel and cut the fruit in pieces. Berries can stay whole.
Stick the pieces of fruit and berries on the skewers.

Life on a stick!

EMPTY THE CUPBOARD BY USING MELTED CHOCOLATE

Puffed rice, coconut flakes, dried cranberries, the last muesli crumbs, and pumpkin seeds are all longing to be covered in chocolate.

CHOCOLATE CANDY

Time: 10 minutes prep

7 oz. dark chocolate or 3 ½ oz. dark chocolate and 3 ½ oz. milk chocolate (200 g/100 +100 g)
5 ⅓ cup seeds, nuts, almonds, dried fruit (800 g)

Melt chocolate in the microwave or in a bowl that is placed on top of a pan with simmering water. Add whatever you like to the chocolate and spread the mass on a dish or in a baking pan with parchment baking paper. Place in the refrigerator and let the chocolate harden. Break into pieces, eat, and enjoy.

Mix any of the following with the chocolate: dried cranberries, yellow or black raisins, pumpkin seeds, walnuts, sunflower seeds, spelt puffs, fired apricots, dried dates, buckwheat puffs, hazelnuts, almonds, rice puffs, pistachios.

Use dark chocolate, milk chocolate, or white chocolate —or mix different kinds.

75

Baked Goods

AT WHAT AGE IS A BAKED CAKE BETTER THAN THE BATTER?

To bake and taste the batter is a real bait for bringing children into the kitchen. Make weekend cakes a new tradition that can replace Saturday candy. Chocolate balls, jelly rolls with Nutella, and freshly baked cinnamon rolls are so much tastier than jelly beans.

CHOCOLATE BALLS

Chocolate balls are made of cacao, coffee, butter, and coconut.

Chocolate balls with colored sprinkles. Dibs on the one with flowers.

CHOCOLATE BALLS

Servings: 16 pieces
Time: 15 minutes prep

3 ½ oz. room-temperature butter (100 g)
2 ½ cup oats (350 g)
½ cup sugar (100 g)
1 tsp vanilla powder (3 g)
¼ cup cacao (50 g)
2 tbsp cold strong coffee or water (30 mL)

GARNISH
⅔ cup coconut flakes or sprinkles (100 g)

Mix all the ingredients. Roll the batter into balls and roll them in coconut flakes or sprinkles. Keep in the refrigerator.

Candy stash
The feeling of pressing your favorite treat into a muffin can only be described with one word: Lovely.

MUFFINS

Preheat oven to: 400° F
Time: 10 minutes prep, 15-20 minutes in the oven

Servings: 10-12 muffin cups

7 oz. room temperature butter (200 g)
1 ½ cup sugar (300 g)
3 eggs
½ cup water (100 mL)
4 cups flour (480 g)
1 ½ tsp baking powder (4 g)

Place the muffin cups in a muffin tin. Whip butter and sugar for a few minutes with an electric mixer. Add one egg at a time and whip. Add water, flour, and baking powder. Whip. Place the batter in the cups. Press down the treat you would like in the batter: fruit, berries, or small candies. Bake in the middle of the oven for 15-20 minutes.

GO FLAVOR HUNTING

Do you have leftover candy canes since Christmas or did the fruit get a little damaged? Chop and add to the batter!

CHOCOLATE MUFFINS

Preheat oven to: 400° F
Time: 15 minutes prep, 15-20
minutes in the oven

Servings: 10-12 muffin cups

3 ½ oz. dark chocolate, in pieces
 (100 g)
7 oz. butter, room temperature
 (200 g)
2 cups sugar (400 g)
4 eggs
2 ½ cup flour (300 g)
½ cup cacao (100 g)
1 tsp baking powder (3 g)
½ tsp vanilla powder (1 g)

Melt the chocolate in a double
boiler and remove from heat. Whip
butter and sugar for a few minutes
with an electric mixer. Add one
egg at a time and whip. Mix the dry
ingredients and then add them to
the butter mixture together with
the chocolate. Place the batter
in the cups. Bake in the middle
of the oven for 15-20 minutes.

Add some glaze and you have a cupcake.

PHILADELPHIA GLAZE ●

1 oz. butter, room temperature (25 g)
7 oz. Philadelphia cream cheese (200 g)
1 cup powdered sugar (200 g)

Whip the butter with an electric mixer until smooth. Add Philadelphia cream cheese and sugar and then whip. Spread the glaze on cooled-off muffins and garnish with pomegranate seeds, crushed Smarties candy, sprinkles, or fresh berries.

MILK CHOCOLATE GLAZE

7 oz. milk chocolate (200 g)

Melt the chocolate in a water bath. Let cool off until the texture thickens. Spread the chocolate on cooled off muffins and top with crushed Smarties, sprinkles, coconut flakes, or fresh berries.

85

CHOCOLATE CUTS OR CHOCOLATE COOKIES

Servings: 35-40 cookies
Preheat oven to: 200°F
Time: 15 minutes prep, 10-25 minutes in the oven

4 cups flour (480 g)
½ cup brown sugar (100 g)
7 oz. butter, room temperature (200 g)
1 egg
⅓ cup cacao (50 g)
3 ½ oz. dark chocolate, chopped (100 g)

1 egg, beaten (optional)
pearl sugar (optional)

Work flour, sugar, butter, egg, and cacao together into a batter, adding the chocolate at the end.

Chocolate cuts: Form 4 lengths as long as the baking sheet. Place them on the sheet with parchment baking paper and flatten. Brush with egg and sprinkle with pearl sugar. Bake for 10-12 minutes. Cut the lengths in diagonal pieces while they are still warm.

Chocolate cookies: Form into 2 lengths, 10 inches long, and cut ½ inch thick cookies. Place on two baking sheets with parchment baking paper and bake for 10-12 minutes per sheet.

INSTANT COOKIE
Always keep a roll of cookie dough in the freezer, ready to slice up and bake. The Lego castle is finally done and has to be celebrated! And here comes grandma to visit, so bring out the rolls!

COCONUT AND LEMON COOKIES

Servings: 35-40 cookies
Preheat oven to: 400° F
Time: 15 minutes prep, 10-25 minutes in the oven

4 cups flour (480 g)
½ cup sugar (100 g)
7 oz. butter, room temperature (200 g)
1 egg
1 ⅓ cup coconut flakes (200 g)
1 ½ lemon, grated zest

1 egg, beaten (optional)
pearl sugar (optional)

Work all the ingredients together into a dough mixture.
  Cuts: Form 4 lengths as long as the baking sheet. Place them on a sheet with parchment baking paper and flatten. Brush with egg and sprinkle with pearl sugar. Bake for 10-12 minutes. Cut the lengths in diagonal cuts while they are still warm.
  Cookies: Form two lengths, 10 inches long, and cut in ½ inch thick cookies. Place on two baking sheet with parchment baking paper and bake for 10-12 minutes per sheet.

Two cookies with ice cream in between = a new pastry

Seven kinds of cookies that are as easy as pie: Add your favorite spices to the rolls.

THIN MUESLI BISCUITS

Servings: About 35 biscuits
Preheat oven to: 350° F
Time: 50 minutes

5 ⅓ oz. butter (150 g)
1 cup sugar (200 g)
1 ⅔ cup flour (200 g)
1 ⅔ cup muesli (250 g)
¼ cup light syrup (50 mL)
2 tbsp water (30 mL)
½ tsp baking powder (1 g)
½ tsp vanilla powder (1 g)

Melt the butter and mix with the rest of the ingredients. Place a tablespoon of batter on the baking sheets with parchment paper, about 9 per sheet. Bake in the middle of the oven until the biscuits have floated out and have a nice color, about 8-10 minutes. Let cool until completely cold.

GRANDMA WARNING
Add wheat germ to the scone batter. It does have a grandma warning to it, but it's oh so juicy and tasty!

*A cake or a bread?
It all depends on
the filling.*

SCONES

Servings: 12 pieces
Preheat oven to: 400° F
Time: 5 minutes prep, 20 minutes in the oven

1 ¼ cup Turkish or Greek yogurt (300 mL)
1 ¼ cup milk (300 mL)
2 eggs
1 ⅓ cup mixed seeds and nuts/almonds (200 g)
⅔ cup dried fruit (100 g)
1 cup wheat germs (150 g)
5 ½ cup sifted spelt flour (600 g)
1 ½ tsp salt (4 g)
4 tsp baking powder (12 g)

Mix yogurt, milk, and eggs in a bowl. Chop nuts/almonds and larger fruit and mix with the rest of the dry ingredients. Mix the fluid with the dry ingredients. Place pieces of parchment baking paper in muffin cups in a muffin form. Bake in the middle of the oven for about 20 minutes.

Some ideas for dried fruit to mix in the scone batter: apple rings, apricots, plums, yellow or black raisins, cranberries, figs, dates. Nuts: hazelnuts, walnuts, pistachios. Seeds: sesame seeds, flax seeds, sunflower seeds, pumpkinseeds, melon seeds.

JELLY ROLL

Servings: About 20 rolls
Preheat oven to: 500° F
Time: 15 minutes prep, 5 minutes in the oven

3 eggs
¾ cup sugar (150 g)
1 ⅔ cup flour (200 g)
1 tsp baking powder (3 g)
2 tbsp hot water (30 mL)

Filling
5 ⅓ oz. blackberries (150 g)
7 oz. raspberry jam (200 g)

Beat eggs and sugar until very fluffy. Add flour, baking powder, and hot water and stir into a smooth batter. Spread the batter on a baking sheet with parchment baking paper and bake immediately for about 5 minutes. Sprinkle sugar over another piece of parchment baking paper and place the baked surface of the cake on the sugar paper. Then pull off the paper that the cake was baked on and let it cool off.

Defrost the blackberries if they were frozen. Mix berries and jam and spread over the entire cake. Roll from one long side to the other and wrap the whole roll in the sugared paper.

You can also fill the jelly roll with vanilla cream and berries, or Nutella.

89

SAY GOODBYE TO DRY BUNS
Sticky dough and long rising time make the best buns in the neighborhood.

Stop buying powder; freshly ground cardamom makes life worth living.

BUNS WITH ALMOND PASTE AND APPLES

Servings: 40 buns
Preheat oven to: 450-500° F
Times: 20 minutes prep, 1 hour of rising and
30 minutes in the oven, about 20 minutes per baking
sheet

2 cups milk (500 mL)
1 oz. yeast (25 g)
½-1 tsp ground cardamom seeds (1-3 g)
½ tsp salt (1 g)
½ cup sugar (100 g)
5 ⅓ oz. butter, room temperature (150 g)
about 10 cups flour (1.2 kg)

Filling
3 ½ oz. butter, room temperature (100 g)
17 ½ oz. almond paste, grated (500 g)
4 apples, peeled, grated

1 egg, beaten
pearl sugar

Heat the milk to 98.6° F. Dissolve the yeast in the milk
and add cardamom, salt, sugar, butter, and flour. Mix
into a smooth and sticky dough, by hand or in a food
processor. Let the dough rise under a baking cloth for
about 1 hour.

   Split the dough in two pieces and roll out one at a
time on a floured table. Spread a layer of butter with
a butter knife. Grate the almond paste over the dough
and apples. Roll up the dough from the long side and
cut in slices about one inch thick. Place the pieces on
a baking sheet with parchment baking paper and let
rise under a baking cloth for about 30 minutes. Brush
with egg and then sprinkle with pearl sugar. Bake in the
middle of the oven for about 10 minutes.

Other fillings:
Butter, cinnamon, and sugar
Butter, vanilla sugar, and sugar
Butter, cardamom, and sugar
Grated almond paste and blueberry jam

Coarsely grated almond paste, apple, and cardamom . . . what a bun!

91

BANANA CAKE

Preheat oven to: 400° F
Time: 20 minutes prep, 30-35 minutes in the oven

1 tbsp butter (15 g)
2 tbsp bread crumbs (30 g)
½ cup raw sugar (100 g)
2 cups powdered sugar (200 g)
5 ⅓ oz. butter, room temperature (150 g)
3 ripe bananas, mixed
½ lemon, juice
2 eggs
2 ½ cup flour (300 g)
1 tsp baking powder (3 g)
1 tsp ground cinnamon (3 g)
½ tsp ground ginger (1 g)
1 ¾ oz. walnuts, chopped (50 g)

GLAZE
7 oz. Philadelphia cream cheese (200 g)
1 oz. butter, melted (25 g)
1 cup powdered sugar (100 g)
½ lemon, grated zest and juice
½ orange, grated zest

Grease a baking pan with butter and bread crumbs. Whip sugar and butter with an electric mixer. Add banana, lemon juice, and eggs into the sugar and butter mixture. Mix all the dry ingredients and add to the batter with the nuts. Pour the batter in the baking pan and bake in the middle of the oven for 30-35 minutes. Turn the cake out of the pan when it has cooled off a little. Let cool until completely cold with the pan on top.

Whip the smooth Philadelphia cream cheese with an electric mixer and add butter, powdered sugar, lemon juice, and lemon zest. An additional option is to garnish with grated lemon zest, nuts, and cinnamon.

The rescue for brown bananas: Bake a banana cake. Another rescue: Peel, slice, and keep in the freezer.

SPICY CRUMBLE PIE WITH APPLES

Servings: 6
Preheat oven to: 450° F
Time: 15 minutes prep, 25 minutes in the oven

CRUMBLE DOUGH
3 ½ oz. butter (100 g)
2 cups oats (250 g)
1 cup pumpkinseeds
3 ½ oz. almond paste, grated (100 g)

1 tbsp butter (15 g)
5 tart apples, peeled and cut in wedges
3 tbsp dark muscovado sugar (45 g)
1-2 tbsp ground cinnamon (10-20 g)
½-1 tbsp cardamom seeds, ground (5-10 g)
1 tsp vanilla powder (3 g)

Mix butter, oats, and pumpkinseeds into a batter and fold the
almond paste into it. Grease a baking pan with butter and place
the apple pieces in it. Spread sugar, cinnamon, cardamom, and
vanilla powder over the apples. Place the crumble dough on top.

   Bake in the middle of the oven until the pie has a nice color,
about 25 minutes. Serve with whipped cream, ice cream, or
vanilla sauce.

CORNFLAKES AND COCONUT PIE WITH BERRIES

Servings: 8
Preheat oven to: 450° F
Time: 10 minutes prep, 15-20 minutes in the oven

1 tbsp butter (15 g)
2 ½ pounds fresh or defrosted berries, like
blackberries and raspberries (1 kg)
¼ cup sugar (50 g)

CRUMBLE DOUGH
3 ½ oz. butter, room temperature (100 g)
½ cup sugar (100 g)
2 ²/3 cup cornflakes (400 g)
²/3 cup coconut flakes (100 g)
¾ cup flour (90 g)

Grease a baking pan with butter. Spread the berries in the pan and sprinkle with sugar. Work the ingredients for the dough together and sprinkle the crumbs over the berries. Bake in the middle of the oven for about 15-20 minutes. Serve with ice cream or vanilla sauce.

A pie made from the summer's berries tastes the best on the dock after a swim. If there is a barbecue grill nearby, you can heat the pan right there.

I wonder how many chocolate balls are needed to master the water?

Relaxing Dinner

COZY START TO THE WEEKEND

Salami, bresaola, parma ham, a few tasty cheeses, and olives. I stop by the deli counter, and then make homemade dips and spreads. The children eat sausages that reach new flavors with a bell pepper dip. Dip, cozy up, and have a relaxing start to a nice weekend!

Who said sausage tastes the best when fried?

DELI PLATTER WITH BELL PEPPER DIP, APPLE DIP, OR TOMATO AND ARTICHOKE SALAD

Things to place on the deli platter: bresaola, parma ham, smoked ham, roast beef, sausage (not fried), salami, brie, blue cheese, manchego, matured cheese, olives, and gherkins.

BELL PEPPER DIP
5 ⅓ oz. grilled marinated bell pepper (weight when drained, 150 g)
⅔ cup almonds (100 g)
1 cup parmesan, pieces (100 g)
2-3 garlic cloves
3 tbsp squeezed lemon (45 mL)
1 red chili, seeded (optional)
½ cup oil (100 mL)
salt and black pepper

Place bell pepper, almonds, parmesan, garlic, squeezed lemon and chili (optional) in a food processor. Mix everything and add the oil while the food processor is working. Add salt and pepper to taste.

APPLE DIP
¾ cup crème fraiche (200 mL)
1 tart apple, peeled, cored, chopped
10 mint leaves, chopped or 2 tbsp (20 g) fresh, grated horseradish
1 lime, juice and grated zest
salt and black pepper

Mix crème fraiche, apple, mint, or horseradish and lime. Add salt and pepper to taste.

TOMATO AND ARTICHOKE SALAD
14 oz. tomatoes, in pieces (400 g)
6 ⅓ oz. marinated artichokes (weight when drained, 150 g), sliced
2 tbsp fresh thyme or 2 tsp dried (20 g/6 g)
1 tbsp white balsamic vinegar (15 mL)
salt flakes and black pepper

Mix tomatoes, artichokes, thyme, and vinegar. Add salt and pepper to taste.

Dip made of grilled bell peppers and almonds, plus a tomato salad with marinated artichokes. Sausage—yum!

Crème fraîche mixed with apples and mint leaves or horseradish with garlic, dill, and feta cheese will save any night.

SHRIMP WITH HERB BREAD AND LEMON AIOLI

Servings: 4
Preheat oven to: 450° F

2 ¼ pounds shrimp, defrosted (1 kg)

HERB BREAD
1 ⅓ cup parsley, chopped (200 g)
2 garlic cloves, finely chopped
1 oz. butter, room temperature (25 g)
1 tbsp olive oil (15 mL)
salt flakes
½ baguette, sliced

Mix parsley, garlic, butter, oil, and salt. Spread the mixture on the baguette slices and bake in the oven for about 10 minutes.

LEMON AIOLI
¾ cup Turkish or Greek yogurt (200 mL)
¼ cup mayonnaise (50 mL)
1 tbsp lemon juice (15 mL)
1 lemon, grated zest
salt flakes and black pepper

Mix yogurt, mayonnaise, lemon juice, and zest. Add salt and pepper to taste.

MAYONNAISE

ervings: 1 ⅔ cup
ime: 10 minutes

egg yolks
tbsp Dijon mustard or sweet mustard (15 mL)
pinches salt (2 mL)
pinch pepper (1 mL)
tbsp squeezed lemon (15 mL)
cup olive oil (200 mL)
cup neutral oil, canola oil (for example) (200 L)

et the ingredients become room temperature.
hip egg yolks, mustard, salt, pepper, and lemon
ith an electric mixer. Continue to whip and add
e oil a little at a time. The mayonnaise should
ave a thick and fluffy texture.

COZY FRIDAY
Possibly the most simple but heavenly tasting dish: Oven-baked cherry tomatoes that are mixed with hot pasta and a lot of parmesan. Thank God for Italy.

PASTA WITH OVEN-BAKED TOMATOES

Servings: 4
Preheat oven to: 300° F
Time: 10 minutes prep, 1 hour in the oven

17 ½ oz. cherry tomatoes (500 g)
2 garlic cloves, sliced
2 tbsp olive oil (30 mL)
salt flakes and black pepper
1 cup black olives (150 g)
17 ½ oz. fresh pasta (500 g)
⅔ cup fresh basil (100 g)
3 ½ oz. parmesan, grated (100 g)
olive oil

Place tomatoes and garlic in a baking pan.
Drizzle oil, salt, and pepper. Bake the tomatoes
for about an hour. Add the olives when there are
about 10 minutes left.

Cook the pasta according to the instructions on
the package. Mix pasta, tomatoes, basil, parmesan, and olive oil. Add salt and pepper to taste.
Serve immediately.

*Homemade is always
the tastiest. Allow the
children in the kitch-
en and make them
miniature chefs.*

CHICKEN ROLLS WITH TOMATOES IN BALSAMIC VINEGAR

Servings: 6
Preheat oven to: 400° F
Time: 10 minutes prep, 30 minutes in the oven

26 ½ oz. cherry tomatoes (750 g)
4 garlic cloves, sliced
½ cup olive oil (100 mL)
¼ cup balsamic vinegar (50 mL)
1 tsp black pepper (3 g)
1 tbsp salt flakes (10 g)
31 ¾ oz. chicken breast filets (900 g)
9 oz. mozzarella, sliced (250 g)
basil leaves

Place tomatoes and garlic in a large baking pan. Add oil and balsamic vinegar. Add salt and pepper. Leave in the oven for 10 minutes. Split the chicken filets to make two thin filets of each. Add salt and pepper to the filets, place one slice of mozzarella and basil leaves, and roll up. Place the chicken rolls on the tomatoes with the seam facing down. Add salt and pepper. Leave for another 20 minutes in the oven. Serve with pasta.

Forgotten tomatoes

Tomatoes that have seen better days come into their own in the oven. Remember to salt and pepper three times: on the tomatoes, in the chicken rolls, and over the whole dish.

SALAMI AND BRIE PIE (TAKE-WHAT-YOU-HAVE PIE)

Servings: 6
Preheat oven to: 450-500° F
Time: 15 minutes prep, 40-50 minutes in the oven

PIE CRUST
2 ½ cup flour or sifted spelt flour (280 g)
4 ½ oz. butter (125 g)
2 tbsp water (30 mL)
½ tsp salt (1 g)

FILLING
1 tbsp butter (15 g)
10 ½ oz. frozen spinach, defrosted (200 g)
½ yellow onion, chopped
salt and black pepper
9 oz. cherry tomatoes (250 g)
2 ½ oz. salami, sliced (75 g)
7 oz. brie, sliced or in pieces (200 g)
3 eggs
1 ²/₃ cup milk (300 mL)
salt and pepper

Make the dough, flatten, and spread it in a spring form, placing the parchment baking paper on the bottom. Place in the freezer for 15 minutes and prebake in the oven at 450° F for 10 minutes.

Heat the butter in a pan, wring the liquid from the spinach, and fry spinach and onions for a few minutes. Add salt and pepper. Place spinach mixture, tomatoes, salami, and brie in the pie crust. Whip egg, milk, salt, and pepper, and pour into the pie crust. Bake in the middle of the oven at 350° F until the egg mixture is firm, about 30-40 minutes.

TAKE-WHAT-YOU-HAVE PIE
Something green from the freezer together with the refrigerator's leftovers and some eggs turn into the best dinner pie of the week.

SAUSAGE IS RIDING THE GRAVY TRAIN TO NEW FLAVORS

Even a little piece of sausage in food can make the most unwilling child soften and suddenly show interest in new flavors. Quality pays off and gives more flavor to even a mild cocktail wiener. A high content of meat, preferably organic and locally produced, is best no matter if the sausage is thin, thick, short, or long.

OVEN BAKED SAUSAGE WITH WARM BEAN AND BELL PEPPER SALAD

Servings: 4
Preheat oven to: 450° F
Time: 25 minutes

4 sausages by choice

BEAN AND BELL PEPPER SALAD
2 tbsp olive oil (30 mL)
2 garlic cloves, pressed
1 yellow or red onion, sliced
1 red chili, seeded and finely chopped
1 ⅓ cup marinated and grilled bell pepper, in pieces (200 g)
1 can cooked kidney beans (13.4 oz./380 g)
1 can cooked black beans (13.4 oz./380 g)
2 tbsp balsamic vinegar (30 mL)
salt
pepper
1 cup parsley, chopped (150 g)

Score the sausages and place them in a baking pan and bake for about 15 minutes.

Heat the oil in a frying pan and fry the onion, chili, and bell pepper for a few minutes. Rinse the beans and drain. Mix beans and balsamic vinegar with the fry-mixture. Let everything get warm and add salt and pepper to taste. Add the parsley. Serve with fried or mashed potatoes.

SAUSAGE RING WITH MEDITERRANEAN FLAVORS

Servings: 6-7
Preheat oven to: 450° F
Time: 10 minutes prep, 20 minutes in the oven

1 sausage ring (2.2 pounds/1 kg)
2 ½ tomatoes, sliced
7 oz. feta cheese, sliced (200 g)
black olives
basil leaves
black pepper
olive oil

Place the sausage ring in a baking pan. Make cuts almost all the way through the sausage. Stick tomato slices, cheese slices, olives, and basil leaves in the cuts. Add pepper and drizzle with olive oil. Bake in the middle of the oven until sausage and cheese has a nice color, about 20 minutes. Serve with mashed potatoes.

Other food to fill the sausage with include: squash slices, grilled bell pepper and mozzarella, apple sliced, dill, and crème fraiche with horseradish.

Sweden's most popular ring
Fill it with any tasty ingredient from the Mediterranean that you can think of. If the flavor directions are different, compromise by filling half of the ring with each.

SAUSAGE SKEWERS

Servings: 4
Time: 15 minutes

**21 oz. sausages of different kinds, in thick
slices or pieces (600 g)
9 oz. cherry tomatoes (250 g)
7 oz. halloumi, pieces (200 g)
2 red bell peppers, pieces
1 yellow squash, slices
basil leaves
olive oil
salt and pepper**

soaked wooden skewers

Stick sausage, vegetables, cheese, and basil
on the skewers. Drizzle with oil and add salt
and pepper. Grill all around, on the barbecue
grill or in the grill pan, until the skewers have
a nice color.

Medium or hot
*The chorizo is complemented
with a milder sausage for the
children. Try lamb sausage.
Add bacon, white button mush-
rooms, bell pepper, and corn.*

TAKE A SHORTCUT

Sometimes fish sticks, a grilled chicken, or maybe even store-bought meatballs are what you need to strike back against a dinner panic. Place the energy on green side dishes instead. Life is full of compromises, so be happy with your choices. The time around the dinner table should be enjoyable and it is totally fine to take a shortcut here and there.

WHEATBERRY WITH FRUIT AND HALLOUMI

Servings: 4
Time: 30 minutes

2 cups water (500 mL)
1 vegetable stock cube
1 ⅓ cup wheatberry (250 g)
1 tbsp olive oil for frying (15 mL)
7 oz. halloumi, in pieces (200 g)
1 pomegranate
1 ⅓ dried apricots, sliced (200 g)
½ red onion, finely chopped
1 lemon, grated zest
2 tbsp squeezed lemon (30 mL)
3 tbsp olive oil (45 mL)
black pepper

Bring water and stock cube to a boil. Add wheat berry and boil under a lid on low heat for about 15 minutes. Let it cool off. Heat the oil and fry the halloumi until it has a nice color. Split the pomegranate into four pieces and remove the seeds. Mix all the ingredients. Eat the salad as it is or together with fried chicken.

Feel free to add other fresh fruit. For example: peach, plum, apple, or replace the pomegranate seeds with another fruit.

PESTO

Time 5 minutes

3 ⅓ cup leafy parsley (500 g)
1 ½-2 cups fresh basil (200-300 g)
3 ½ oz. parmesan, grated (100 g)
2 garlic cloves
½ cup olive oil (100 mL)
½ tsp salt (1 g)
black pepper

Mix the parsley, basil, parmesan, nuts, and garlic in a mixer or food processor. Add the oil while mixing. Add salt and pepper to taste.

TOMATO SOUP

Servings: 2
Time: 15 minutes

1 tbsp olive oil (15 mL)
1 garlic clove, sliced
½ yellow onion, chopped
1 chicken or vegetable stock cube
1 can crushed tomatoes (14 oz./400 g)
½ cup water (100 mL)
2 pinches salt (2 mL)
black pepper
1 tsp sugar (3 g)
½ cup cream (100 mL)

SIDES
pesto, bought or homemade
roasted seeds
bread, for example the cheese bread on
p. 132

Heat the oil in a pan. Fry the onion for a minute without bringing color to it. Add the stock cube, tomatoes, water, salt, pepper, and sugar. Let it boil for 5 minutes. Add cream and mix the soup until smooth. Serve with pesto, roasted seeds, and bread.

SOUP KITCHEN HEAT
Tomato soup with pesto, seeds, and cheese bread.

ONION SOUP

Servings: 4
Preheat oven to: 500 °F
Time: 30 minutes-1 hour

2 tbsp butter (30 g)
6 yellow and red onions, sliced
2 bay laurel leaves
1 tsp dried thyme (3 g)
1 tsp dried oregano (3 g)
2 vegetable stock cubes
1 quart water (1 liter)
¾ cup water (200 mL)
1 tsp salt (3 g)
½ tsp black pepper (1 g)

3 slices bread, toasted
3 ½ oz. aged cheese (100 g)
fresh thyme (optional)

Heat the butter in a pot and fry the onion for a few minutes. Add the rest of the ingredients for the soup and bring to a boil. Let simmer for at least 15 minutes; preferably 45 minutes if you have the time. Cut the bread into cubes. Pour the soup into oven-safe bowls, add bread cubes, and sprinkle with cheese. Sprinkle with fresh thyme if you want to. Bake in the oven until the cheese has melted and has a nice color.

BROCCOLI SOUP WITH FETA CHEESE

Servings: 4
Time: 20 minutes

24 ¾ oz. broccoli (700 g)
2 tbsp butter (30 g)
1 leek, chopped
2 chicken or vegetable stock cubes
1 quart water (1 liter)
1 bay laurel leaf
½ cup cream (100 mL)
salt
pepper

Slice the coarse broccoli stems and split the broccoli into smaller florets. Heat the butter in a large pan and fry the onion and broccoli stems for a couple of minutes. Add florets, stock cubes, water, and bay laurel. Simmer while covered for about 7 minutes. Remove the soup from the heat, take out the bay laurel leaf, and add cream. Add salt and pepper to taste. Serve the soup with feta cheese.

ADD SOMETHING TO THE SOUP
Bring company for the soup and make it even more filling with:
Fried bacon
Croutons made from bread that turned too dry
Roasted nuts and seeds
Pasta
Feta cheese

You can blend the vegetables until they are no longer recognizable—this usually makes those who stubbornly oppose vegetables start slurping.

CARROT SOUP WITH CROUTONS

Servings: 4
Time: 30 minutes

1 oz. butter (25 g)
28 ¼ oz. carrots, sliced (800 g)
1 yellow onion, in pieces
1 garlic clove, chopped
2 chicken or vegetable stock cubes
3 ½ cup water (800 mL)
½ orange, grated zest
½ cup squeezed orange
1 tsp fresh ginger, grated (3 g)
salt
pepper

CROUTONS
olive oil
2-3 slices soft bread
salt flakes
pepper

Heat the butter in a large pan. Fry carrots and onion for a few minutes. Add stock cubes and water and bring to a boil until the carrots are soft, about 5-15 minutes depending on the season and size. Remove the pan from the heat, add cream, and mix the soup with a hand blender, making a smooth consistency. Add orange, ginger, salt, and pepper to taste.

CROUTONS
Cut the bread in cubes. Heat oil in a frying pan and fry the bread cubes until crispy. Add salt and pepper. Serve with the soup.

GINGER STIR-FRY

Servings: 4-6
Time: 15 minutes

¼ cup sunflower oil or other neutral oil
  (60 mL)
3 garlic cloves, sliced
1 red chili, seeded, sliced
1 tbsp fresh ginger (10 g)
½ cauliflower head, florets
5 ⅓ oz. sugar snaps, sliced (150 g)
4-5 leeks, sliced
¼ head Savoy or Chinese cabbage,
  sliced
1 cup unsalted cashew nuts
1 lime, juiced
½ tbsp salt flakes (5 g)

Allow the oil to become very hot in a wok
pan. Fry garlic, chili, and ginger for about
a minute. Add the cauliflower and wok for
a few minutes. Add sugar snaps, leeks,
cabbage, and nuts and wok for another
minute. Add lime and salt to taste.

   Serve as an alternative to rice, pasta,
or potatoes, with fried chicken, minced
meat, fish, pork chops, or beef.

Make ginger stir-fry
in a wok and you will
have amazing flavor
with your fish.

WHITE CABBAGE IN THE OVEN

Preheat oven to: 450° F
Time: 5 minutes prep, 15-20 minutes in the oven

½ **white cabbage head**
1 tbsp salt flakes (10 g)
1 tbsp liquid honey (15 mL)
2 tbsp olive oil (30 mL)
black pepper
½ **tbsp fresh ginger, grated, or 1 tsp dried
    (5 g/3 g)**

Remove the stem and cut the white cabbage into several large pieces. Place the pieces in a baking pan and add the rest of the ingredients. Stir everything around with your hands. Leave in the oven until the cabbage is soft, about 15-20 minutes. Serve as an alternative to salad.

Cabbage is cool
Salad is cold as ice during the winter. Move over to a warm alternative with cabbage that is baked until soft in the oven.

CARROT SALAD

Time: 5 minutes

14 oz. carrots, grated (400 g)
²/₃ cup sesame seeds (100 g)
1 lime, grated zest and juice
1 tbsp oil (15 mL)
salt and black pepper

Mix carrots, sesame seeds, lime, and olive oil.
Add salt and pepper to taste.

Large, small, white, red, or black as night, all you have to do is browse the bean shelves. If you want to be on the safe side, chickpeas are always a favorite.

BEAN SALAD WITH SUN-DRIED TOMATOES

Servings: 6
Time: 5 minutes

1 package (14 oz.) cooked kidney beans (400 g)
1 package (14 oz.) cooked chickpeas (400 g)
¼ cup olive oil (50 mL)
¼ cup balsamic vinegar (50 mL)
1 tsp salt (3 g)
½ tsp black pepper (1 g)

1 red onion, finely chopped
about 8 marinated sun-dried tomatoes, sliced (75 g)
⅓ cup fresh basil, chopped (50 g)

Rinse the beans in cold water and drain well. Mix oil, vinegar, honey, salt, and pepper. Mix beans, vinaigrette, onion, tomatoes, and basil.

Serve as an alternative to a green salad or instead of potatoes, rice, or pasta.

Snacks

CHEESE AND HAM OR HAM AND CHEESE?

A snack easily becomes a sandwich empty of energy. Bring new life into the food in between your meals. Nuts, dried fruit, frozen berries, yogurt, carrots, and tortilla chips are good items to keep on hand. Apple compote with yogurt and coconut flakes can be had more than once and quesadillas are something entirely different than a regular sandwich.

A RICH TOAST
A whole-grain bread and a topping of bananas
and cottage cheese make this toast anything but
poor. Yummy snack.

RICH FRENCH TOAST

Servings: 4
Time: 10 minutes

½ cup milk
2 eggs
1 tsp ground cinnamon (3 g)
4 slices bread or sourdough bread
2 tbsp butter (30 g)

9 oz. cottage cheese (250 g)
8 oz. mixed berries (225 g)
1-2 bananas, sliced (optional)
1 ¾ oz. hazelnuts, chopped (50 g)

Beat eggs, milk, and cinnamon. Turn the bread
slice in the egg mixture. Heat the butter in a
frying pan and fry the slices on both sides until
golden brown. Serve with cottage cheese, berries, or bananas and nuts.

Adult toast: Add 1 cup grated parmesan and
chopped basil in the egg and milk mixture. Fry
according to above and serve with sour cream or
crème fraiche, finely chopped red onion, and roe.

QUESADILLAS

Servings: 4
Time: 10 minutes

2 ½ oz. salami, chopped (75 g)
7 oz. brie, chopped (200 g)
1 red bell pepper, chopped
fresh thyme
4 soft tortilla breads

Mix salami, cheese, bell pepper, and thyme in a bowl. Spread sausage and cheese mixture in half of the bread. Fold the empty halves over the rest and press until they stick to each other. Heat a dry frying pan and fry both sides until the cheese has melted, about 1-2 minutes.

TEX-MEX SANDWICH
A tortilla and some imagination make up this sandwich. Empty the refrigerator of leftovers, grate some cheese, and heat in a frying pan.

Yogurt and muesli are filling topping tips.

PEAR COMPOTE WITH GINGER

Servings: 4
Time: 15 minutes

2 ½ pounds pears, peeled, in pieces (1 kg)
½ cup water (100 mL)
¼ cup sugar (50 g)
½-1 tbsp fresh ginger, grated (5-10 g)
2 tbsp squeezed lemon (30 mL)

Mix all the ingredients in a pan and cook on medium heat until almost all the fluid has evaporated. Serve with a spoonful of Turkish or Greek yogurt and chopped nuts.

Garnish with seeds or muesli instead of nuts.

121

PINK SMOOTHIE

Servings: 2-3 glasses
Time: 2 minutes

1 ¼ cup plain yogurt (300 mL)
3 ½ oz. frozen raspberries (100 g)
5 ⅓ oz. frozen mango (150 g)

Mix the ingredients and pour into
  glasses.

SMOOTHIE STASH
Save the leftovers of the fruit
bowl: Cut into pieces and freeze
for future smoothies.

122

Drink a fruit
Do not miss the simplest snack of all. Mix a smoothie and all of a sudden, your energy returns.

DARK BLUE SMOOTHIE

Servings: 2-3 glasses
Time: 2 minutes

3 ⅓ cup blackberries or black currant Proviva drink (780 mL)
8 oz. frozen blueberries (225 g)
½ tsp vanilla powder (1 g)

Mix the ingredients and pour into glasses.

LIGHT YELLOW SMOOTHIE

Servings: 2-3 glasses
Time: 2 minutes

1 ¼ cup vanilla yogurt
1 large ripe banana
⅔-¾ cup squeezed orange (150-200 mL)

Mix ingredients and pour into glasses.

SOS: WE NEED EMERGENCY RATIONS
In distress there is no law, and in an SOS situation, you'll do anything to avoid a catastrophe. But emergency rations should at least be moderately tasty. Toasted bread with butter or plain macaroni? Forget about it. Whole grain crisp bread with butter, plain yogurt, and cucumber or carrot sticks are what I call emergency food. Nothing to long for, but definitely edible.

MELON WITH SALT FLAKES AND FENNEL

Time: 5 minutes

2 tbsp fennel seeds (20 g)
2 tbsp salt flakes (20 g)
1 watermelon

Roast the fennel seeds in a dry, hot frying pan. Mix salt flakes and fennel seeds. Cut the melon into smaller pieces and place on a large dish.

STIR-FRIED FRUIT

Servings: 4
Time: 10 minutes

1 quart pineapples and peaches (1 liter)
¾ oz. butter (20 g)
2 tbsp honey (30 mL)
2 tsp fresh ginger, grated (6 g)

Remove peel and core from the pineapple and cut the pulp into pieces. Split the peaches, remove the pits, and cut the fruit in pieces. Heat butter, honey, and ginger in a wok pan. Add the fruit when the wok pan is very hot. Only fry until the wok is warm.

Serve with ice cream or whipped cream.

Vitamin bomb
The best kick for a student: orange salad with pistachios, cardamom, pomegranate seeds, and honey.

ORANGE SALAD

Servings: 4
Time: 10 minutes

6 oranges
1 pomegranate
1 tsp cardamom seeds, ground (3 g)
2/3 cup unsalted pistachios, chopped (100 g)
2 tbsp liquid honey (30 mL)
optionally mint leaves

Remove the peel from the orange with a small, sharp knife. Then cut out wedges without the skin and remove the seeds. Place the orange wedges on a large plate or in a bowl. Spread the pomegranate seeds, cardamom, and nuts over the oranges. Drizzle over honey and garnish with mint leaves.

REFUSE DRY CRUMBLES

Important insider-tips: 1 ¾ oz. yeast for ¼ cup water is not OK.
Use a half package of yeast max, preferably a quarter, and
longer risingtime is the key. Take care of the dough when you
have the time and I guarantee you will have a wonderful and
moist bread, free from yeast flavor.

BISCUITS IN A BAKING PAN

Servings: 8 loaves
Preheat oven to: 400° F
Time: 5 minutes prep, rising time
1 ½-2 ½ hours, 40 minutes in oven

1 ¾ butter (50 g)
1 ¼ cup sour milk
¾ cups water (200 mL)
1 oz. yeast (25 g)
2 tsp salt (10 mL)
¼ cup dark syrup (50 mL)
1 tsp whole anise, ground (3 g)
1 tsp whole fennel, ground (3 g)
8 ⅔ cups sifted rye flour (1 kg)

Melt the butter and mix with the sour milk and water in a bowl. Crumble the yeast and dissolve it into the liquid. Add the rest of the ingredients and stir into a fairly sticky dough. Leave to rise under a baking cloth for at least one hour, preferably two.

Place parchment baking paper in a small baking pan, 8 x 12 inches, and cover the bottom with the dough. Flatten the dough with floured hands and cut out eight pieces. Rise under a baking cloth for 30 minutes. Bake in the middle of the oven for about 40 minutes.

HAMBURGER ROLLS

Servings: 12 pieces
Preheat oven to: 450° F
Time: 10 minutes prep, 1 ½ hours of rising time, 15 minutes in the oven

1 oz. yeast (25 g)
2 cups water (500 mL)
1 tbsp honey (15 mL)
2 tsp salt (6 g)
9 cups sifted spelt flour (1 kg)
⅓ cup wheat bran (50 g)

BRUSHING AND GARNISH
1 egg, beaten
sesame seeds

Dissolve the yeast in the water, add the rest of the ingredients, and mix into a loose dough. Rise under a baking cloth for one hour.

   Place the dough on a floured table and knead it. Roll out the dough into one or two lengths and then split the lengths into 12 pieces. Flatten each piece with floured hands and place them on baking sheets with parchment baking paper. Brush with egg and sprinkle with sesame seeds. Let rise for 30 minutes without a baking cloth. Bake in the middle of the oven for about 15 minutes.

CHEESE BREAD

Servings: 8 loaves
Preheat oven to: 450-500° F
Time: 5 minutes prep, 2 hours of rising time, about 20 minutes in the oven

⅓ oz. yeast (10 g)
1 cup water (250 mL)
½ cup neutral yogurt (100 mL)
⅔ cup oats (100 g)
1 tsp salt (3 g)
5 ½ cup sifted spelt flour (600 g)
2 ½ oz. aged cheese, grated (75 g)

Dissolve the yeast into water. Add yogurt, oats, salt, and sifted spelt and mix into a sticky dough. Place parchment baking paper in a small baking pan, about 8 x 12 inches.

Roll the dough into a length on a floured table, cut 8 pieces, and place them in the baking pan. Brush with some water and sprinkle with cheese. Let rise under a baking cloth for 2 hours. Bake at 450° F for about 20 minutes. You can also increase the heat the last 5 minutes if the cheese does not already have a golden color. Serve with the tomato soup from p. 110.

SLOW FERMENTED BREAKFAST BUNS

Night shift
Let the dough rise overnight and wake up and surprise the family with freshly baked breakfast buns.

Servings: 20 buns
Preheat oven to: 500° F
Time: 10 minutes prep, 12 hours of rising time (overnight), 15 minutes in the oven

1 oz. yeast (25 g)
2 cups water (500 mL)
2/3 cups wheat germ (100 g)
2 tsp salt (6 g)
8 cups flour (960 g)

olive oil
about 2/3 cup sunflower seeds (100 g)

Dissolve the yeast in the water. Mix with the rest of the ingredients into a sticky batter. Grease your hands with olive oil and form small buns from the dough. Place the buns on a baking sheet with parchment baking paper, either close together on one sheet or more wide apart on two sheets. Sprinkle with sunflower seeds. Place a baking cloth over the breads and place in the refrigerator. Let it sit overnight.

Take out the sheet or sheets the next morning and leave them at room temperature for 30 minutes. Bake in the middle of the oven for about 15 minutes.

TWISTED BAGUETTES

Servings: 8 baguettes
Preheat oven to: 450-500° F
Time: 10 minutes prep, 2-4 hours rising
time, 20-25 minutes in the oven

1 oz. yeast (25 g)
1 quart lukewarm water (1 liter)
17 ⅓ cup sifted spelt flour (1.8 kg)
4 cups flour (480 g)
1 tbsp salt (10 g)
2 tbsp live oil (30 mL)

BRUSHING AND GARNISH
1 egg, beaten
sunflower seeds and pumpkin seeds or
rosemary and salt flakes

Dissolve yeast in the lukewarm water in a
large bowl. Add sifted spelt, flour, salt, and
olive oil and mix into a sticky dough. Let the
dough rise for two hours under a baking
cloth, preferably for four hours if there is
time.

Place the dough on a well floured table.
Split the dough into eight pieces and form into
baguettes. Move the right hand from you and
the left hand to you when you roll the baguettes
in order to twist them. Place the baguettes on
baking sheets with parchment baking paper.
Brush with egg, sprinkle with seeds or rosemary, and add salt flakes. Let it rise without a
baking cloth for about 30 minutes.

Bake the bread at 500° F for 15 minutes,
then reduce the temperature to 450° F and
bake for another 5-10 minutes.

APPRECIATE THE MESS
Many dough recipes in this book are
probably stickier than you are used to,
but less yeast means more time to rise.

INDEX